ALL

Stephen Curry

Anthony Curcio

BLUE
RIVER
PRESS

Indianapolis, Indiana

Published by Blue River Press
Indianapolis, Indiana
www.brpressbooks.com

Distributed by Cardinal Publishers Group
A Tom Doherty Company, Inc.
www.cardinalpub.com

ISBN: 978-1-68157-174-4

Cover Design: David Miles
Book Design: Rick Korab, Korab Company Design
Cover Artist: Anna Wagoner
Editor: Dani McCormick
Illustrator: Amber Calderon, Colleen Deignan

Printed in the United States of America

10 9 8 7 6 5 4 3 2 1   20 21 22 23 24 25 26 27 28

CONTENTS

ALL ABOUT

The greatest shooter in NBA history entered his first high school basketball game standing only five feet, six inches tall and weighing 130 lbs. The tiny guard made up with skill what he lacked in size and eventually became his school's all-time leading scorer, earning All-State honors, but still would not be offered a single Division 1 college scholarship even after growing several inches. The many college recruiters, coaches and scouts who came to watch the undersized three-point-shooting guard were so focused on what he didn't have that they missed the very important things that he did.

Except for one. Bob McKillop, the head coach for the Davidson Wildcats. McKillop was able to see in Stephen what no one else could. Over the years, Curry made up for his size by learning to shoot higher, faster, and with range never before seen. The next year, Stephen led the small, 2,000 student body school to the Elite 8, where his spectacular performances against schools ten times Davidson's size would make Stephen Curry a household name.

The Golden State Warriors drafted Stephen with the 7th pick in the 2009 NBA Draft. After an impressive rookie season, Curry suffered from a string of recurring ankle injuries that nearly threatened his career. With the addition of head coach Steve Kerr, which designed a team offense around Stephen's strength's, and Stephen remaining healthy, the Golden State Warriors became a dominant force, first in the Western Conference, then taking downing the powerhouse Cleveland Cavaliers led by superstar LeBron James. Stephen would win his first MVP, along with shattering all season three-point records, hitting a total of 402 for the season. The following year, Curry would make history again by winning the first-ever unanimous MVP selection.

CHAPTER ONE

Growing Up Curry

Half a century ago, Wardell 'Jack' Curry installed a basketball hoop in his backyard using an old utility pole, a fiberglass backboard, and some steel brackets. Little did he know that this dingy homemade hoop would train a family of NBA stars. Jack and his wife Juanita had five children,

Dell was known for his "instant 0," which is basketball slang for a player (typically not in the starting five), who can enter a basketball game and help his team score immediately. Dell was so good at this that he won the NBA's Sixth Man of the Year award for his play in the 1993 - 94 season.

but it was their only son Dell for which this hoop was intended. Due to the ground it stood in, every shot on the hoop required exact precision to keep it upright, which created Dell's fluid, deadly jumper—a shot that produced a state title, a scholarship to Virginia Tech, and a 16-year NBA career.

During her school-age years, Sonya Curry (then Adams) excelled in athletics and academics. Since that time, she has helped not just her own children succeed but others too—by starting (and running) her own elementary school! She was even the school's principal.

Dell graduated as his high school's all-time leading scorer, a McDonald's All-American, and was headed to Virginia Tech University on a basketball scholarship. Dell would later be introduced to Sonya Adams by a mutual friend. Sonya was a five-foot, five-inch volleyball player who had been the Virginia Defensive Player of the Year in high school prior to receiving an athletic scholarship as well. The two began dating prior to Dell's senior year, when he was named a first-team All-American after averaging 24.1 points per game and leading Virginia Tech to the NCAA Tournament. The school would honor their second all-time leading scorer by retiring Dell's number thirty jersey.

It would be no surprise that Stephen has been around basketball his entire life, considering when his dad would say "I'm leaving for work" meant that he was leaving to go play basketball!

Dell Curry was selected by the Utah Jazz with the fifteenth overall pick in the 1986 NBA Draft. After his first season, Dell was traded to Cleveland, where Sonya joined him, and the two married. Shortly after news the couple were expecting a baby, Dell was selected to a new team. The Charlotte Hornets were literally a new team, an NBA expansion team. Expansion teams like the 1988 Hornets, had to start from scratch by designing a new logo, creating a new mascot, hiring a new coach, finding players, etc.

On March 14, 1988, Wardell Stephen Curry II was born in Akron, Ohio. Ironically just a few years earlier, future NBA superstar LeBron James had been born in the same city, and hospital! However, little Stephen

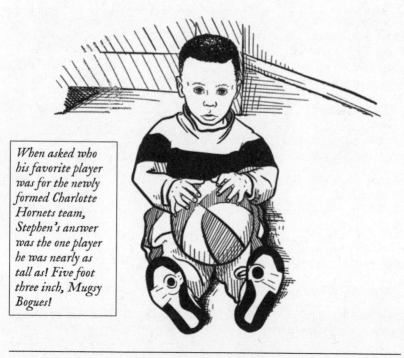

When asked who his favorite player was for the newly formed Charlotte Hornets team, Stephen's answer was the one player he was nearly as tall as! Five foot three inch, Mugsy Bogues!

wouldn't stay in Ohio long. Before his first birthday, the young family would be settled in Charlotte, North Carolina. Before his third, Stephen would have a baby brother named Seth Adham Curry.

Despite his dad playing in the NBA, Steph was not immediately drawn to basketball. Instead, he spent his childhood playing all kinds of sports. He played football, baseball, soccer, and even golf! In fact, Dell even had a special golf club cut down to Steph's size so that he could ride the carts and play alongside him! The most important thing to Sonya and Dell was not about how good their kids would become in sports but how good of people their kids would become. This was so important to the Currys that Sonya even started a school to better guide their young sons and daughter, Sydel Alicia Curry. All three would attend Christian Montessori School of Lake Norman, a school that Sonya still runs.

Little Stephen had been around basketball since he was born, trying to pick up the basketball and mimic what his father would do during warmups. Sonya signed up six-year-old Stephen to play on a team made up of seven-, eight-, and nine-year-olds.

Stephen played many sports growing up. His second favorite (to basketball of course!) was baseball. Dell was a star pitcher in baseball as well, being drafted by the Texas Rangers in the 1982 draft!

The young players named the team The Stars. The team was very good, and so was their six-year-old point guard who could out-dribble and out-shoot most adults. The Stars advanced through the state and interstate tournaments, finding themselves in Orlando playing for the ten-and-under National Championships! The Stars were playing against a team from Pennsylvania called the Potomac Valley Blue Devils. The Blue Devils had a three-point lead with only a few seconds left in the game. Stephen was purposely fouled shooting a game-tying three-pointer. He now had to make all three free throws to tie the game. Little Stephen took a deep breath then fired off his first shot. He missed. The Stars lost the National Championship. Stephen was devastated.

"It was a moment that defined my childhood. It was all I thought about for a year. I felt I could go one of two ways afterward. I could run from that moment, or I could want it again." Stephen later told Sports Illustrated magazine. "I decided I wanted it."

In the early 1990's, Stephen starred in two Burger King commercials with his dad! During the TV ad, the two are walking in the park and Dell looks down at Stephen and asks him what he wants to be when he grows up, "I want to be a professional basketball player." Dell responds by saying, "Boy, that's going to take a lot of hard work and practice..."

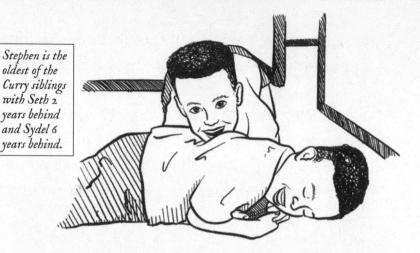

Stephen is the oldest of the Curry siblings with Seth 2 years behind and Sydel 6 years behind.

Stephen Curry wasn't born with game. He was the opposite of big, tall, or strong. He also wasn't especially fast. Steph's skill on the court started like anyone else's would—no knowledge combined with zero skill. Only with hours and hours of practice, much of it on Grandpa Jack's beat-up hoop, would Stephen begin to develop some skill. He would throw up brick after brick on that old hoop, forcing him to chase after the ball just to do it all over again. A miss on Grandpa Jack's court usually meant a ball covered with mud. Before Stephen was ever able to make ten-in-a-row on that hoop, he had to first hear a thousand clangs off the rim and dirty a hundred shirts. This would be enough to become a good player in grade school. To be more, a player must improve. Stephen took a step back when shooting, then another.

Stephen was an excellent student and always looked for a way to improve. His dad worked through drills with him, and he practiced game-winners as his grandma counted down seconds. He listened to point guard Chris Paul at the summer camps he attended, and played his little brother Seth one-on-

Although Sonya believed in Stephen and his dreams to play professionally, it was much more important to her to raise a good person rather than a good basketball player. She famously grounded him - not letting him play in a game - because Stephen wasn't helping around the house or doing his chores!

one for hours. He watched his favorite players on TV. Stephen was always studying.

No one had to tell Stephen to practice hours a day. Stephen's passion was basketball. He loved it. "From Virginia Tech University, starting at guard for the Chicago Bulls, number thirty Stephen Curry!" he imagined the announcer calling before his future NBA game. Basketball was Stephen's love and playing at Virginia Tech and later in the NBA was his dream.

CHAPTER TWO

Don't Shoot from the Hip

"I was about ten years old, and our AAU team drove down to Charlotte to play," future teammate of Steph and NBA star Kevin Durant remembers.

"I walk in the gym and this guy's stepping across half court just pulling jump shots," Durant said. "Splash. Splash. And when we played him, he had like thirty-five jump shots, and he was like ten years old. I was like, who is this? And ten years later . . . that was Steph Curry."

After ten seasons spent in Charlotte, Dell's contract was up. He was the last remaining player from the original Hornets team and, at thirty-five years old, he was well past NBA retirement age. However, shooting an NBA-best 47.6% three-point accuracy would lead to a three-year contract with the Toronto Raptors.

In Canada, the Curry children would attend Queensway Christian College. The small school taught students from kindergarten through twelfth grade. The faith-based school had under two-hundred kids, meaning basketball tryouts was more just a matter of showing up. Both Steph and Seth were on the same team. Seth would dribble the ball up court and pass to Steph, who usually did the

Both Curry brothers would later follow in their dad's footsteps to the NBA.

rest, frequently scoring forty or more points during a game despite being the smallest player.

There was a minute left in the championship game and Queensway trailed Hilcrest Junior, a larger public school, by six points. Players huddled around Coach James Lackey, who also taught history for the school. The coach didn't have a play. They had struggled against Hilcrest all game, and Lackey now struggled with what to say.

"Give me the ball," came from the back of the huddle. All the players turned, looking at Stephen, who was now waiting for Coach Lackey's approval. The coach paused, knowing that giving the ball to one player and telling the other four to get out of his way was not at all a good example of teamwork. The buzzer sounded. He was out of time.

"Give him the ball and get out of his way," the coach said.

Two quick three-pointers by the small Curry rattled Hilcrest so bad that the team fell apart. Queensway won by six!

"I've never seen anything like it," Coach Lackey said, "We ended up winning the game . . . and it was entirely because of Stephen."

Steph was such a good shot, he frequently won games of H-O-R-S-E against his father's teammates. Raptor players Vince Carter, Tracy McGrady, and Mark Jackson all remember playing young Steph. His parents knew he needed more competition than the small Queensway league could offer. Stephen later joined a Toronto select team called the Five-Oh. The team played in a league known for producing high school stars and a few NBA players as well.

It was while playing with the Five-Oh that Stephen first remembered being in a 'zone' for the first time.

Stephen's time on the 5 - 0 team allowed him to develop his NBA mindset and really begin to stand out.

"I shot everywhere, and I couldn't miss."

He scored 63 points in the game that day, and his dad couldn't get out of there fast enough. Dell got up from the bleachers and walked out of the gym.

"All these people were coming in to see what was going on, and was so much commotion, it seemed like he was never going to stop," Dell remembered of the day.

"I had to get out of there. I felt bad for the other team. I couldn't watch what he was doing to those kids."

Prior to arriving in Charlotte, the Curry family was always on the move – following Dell as he was traded to/from NBA teams.

When his third season in Toronto came to an end, Dell Curry announced that he was retiring from the NBA after sixteen seasons. The Currys moved back to Charlotte, North Carolina where Stephen continued playing select-level basketball. His rival in the city's competitive AAU league was a kid named CJ Young.

"He was a physical specimen who had speed, athleticism. . . . CJ was a monster," Stephen remembered. CJ couldn't shoot like Steph, but he was the more complete player. The small and skinny

Steph was more often than not, the smallest player on his team. He was 5'6" and 125 pounds as a sophomore in high school.

Stephen was easily shoved aside and mowed over when facing CJ's team, "I was clearly overmatched." With a determination never to back down, the frail and frustrated young Steph started to fight back.

"My ribs would be so sore after playing, from Steph elbowing me," Young would say. In a way, Steph had earned CJ's respect.

The years spent getting thrown around by larger players like CJ would one day have its value.

As a freshman at Charlotte Christian High School, Steph was only five feet, six inches tall. He was so small his number thirty jersey hardly stayed on his shoulders, so he took number twenty that was a size smaller. His coaches decided to put him on the Junior Varsity team to give him another year to prepare for Varsity basketball. "My freshman year, I went through some doubts about whether I could play on the varsity level." Curry said about his first two years in high school, a time when he wasn't very confident. Stephen's first taste of varsity basketball came when he was subbed in late in the fourth quarter of a game. There was a little time left and the Charlotte Christian Knights were trailing by eleven points. He got the ball and dribbled across half court, where he met his defender. A quick crossover, and Stephen hit a three. Stephen had hardly played a minute in the game, but it had been more than enough for the Knights' coaches to put him on the varsity squad.

Besides fighting back against CJ on the court, Stephen was kind to everyone and very respectful. Because of this, most everyone like Stephen, but there were a few kids that were also very jealous of

Despite playing 82 games a year, Dell managed to spend time and work with Stephen for many years.

the NBA star's son, who seemed to have it all. Just like adults, kids can say things just to hurt others. "You'll never be as good as your dad," and "You're only five-eight, you can't play in the NBA," were among some of the things Stephen heard. The young star began doubting himself and his basketball future. He started to shy away from the end of game and the high-pressure moments that he had once craved.

Stephen was still trying to figure a lot of this out his sophomore year at Charlotte Christian. His passion to play the game wasn't going away so Stephen talked to his parents. His mom encouraged him to just be himself and ignore what everyone else says. His dad agreed and talked to him about his goal of playing college ball. They discussed his shooting technique. Stephen was still shooting from his waist, which was a common trait for shorter, weaker players that need the power to get the proper arc to drop into a ten-foot hoop.

"We were talking about it, and we knew I had to get my shot off a lot quicker when playing at the varsity level," Stephen would say. "My shot was a kind of a fling from the hip type of deal." Knowing players at higher levels would block his shot, Dell worked with Stephen on changing his form. This task however, was a daunting one. To completely change the way a player has been shooting a basketball for ten years is comparable to asking someone to change the way they walk.

"It was tough for me to watch: them in the backyard, late nights, a lot of hours during the day, working on his shot," his brother Seth remembers. Fueled by his dream to play for Virginia Tech, Stephen would stay outside for hours, taking shot after shot. "They broke it down to a point where he couldn't shoot at all. He'd be back there at times crying, not wanting to work on his game."

He went from being able to consistently make twenty-foot shots, to barely getting the ball in from ten. "I couldn't get the strength to shoot outside the paint," remembered Steph. Although it felt like it never was going to work, eventually it did. "Finally, I started to get it. It started to click." Steph says with a smile. Changing his form came with an expense, "it was the worst summer of my childhood," he added.

"Thankfully, I figured it out right in time for our

basketball season." Almost immediately Stephen resumed the brilliance on the court he once had. "He had to do it rep, after rep, after rep, to a point where he was able to master it," Dell recalled.

Changing his shot paid off. That upcoming season and the one after, Stephen would earn All-Conference and All-State honors, leading the Knights to the state tournament. He ended his career at Charlotte Christian as the Knights' all-time leading scorer.

The number thirty that Stephen has worn his entire career is in honor of his dad, Dell, who wore the number as well.

CHAPTER THREE

Coach Bob

Stephen had waited years for this time to come. He had already toured the Virginia Tech (sometimes called the "Hokie") campus and met assistant coaches who scouted his games. Now he was just waiting on the scholarship offer to play on the VT basketball team. He didn't know exactly when the letter would come or the phone would ring, but it would be soon.

"When you see them at all your games and practices, you think something good's going to happen." explained Steph of the Hokie's initial interest. But nothing happened. There would be no offer from his parent's alma mater, Virginia Tech.

In fact, not one major Division One program made Stephen an offer.

Many coaches had never heard about Stephen, and others didn't think he was worth the time.

Stephen was told he was too small, too weak, and he just wasn't good enough to play division I basketball.

"I don't ever remember even seeing him," admitted Roy Williams, who was head coach of the University of North Carolina, just a two-hour drive from Charlotte Christian High School. Other coaches would see Stephen play and despite his amazing ability, could not look past his small frame and boyish appearance. "I do know that when I did see him I thought, 'Man, he is little,'" added Williams.

One coach, like others, had noticed how well Curry shot the ball, but, unlike other coaches, also noticed how hard he worked, his passion and determination, and that he never gave up. His name was Bob McKillop, and he was the head basketball coach at Davidson College, a small school with under 1,800 students, but that often competes against teams from schools ten-times their size.

Stephen was only ten years old when Coach McKillop first saw him play, and it was on the baseball field! Stephen played centerfield on the same little league teams as McKillop's son.

Later, Coach McKillop drove to the

The best advice Stephen ever received: "Steph, I'm only going to tell you this one time. After that, this basketball dream... it's going to be what it's going to be. But here's what I'll say: NO ONE gets to write your story but you. Not some scoutes. Not some tournament. Not these other kids..."

Curry's home to offer Stephen a four-year basketball scholarship to Davidson College. Sonya reassured the coach as he was leaving, "Don't worry coach, I'm going to fatten him up for you."

"I'll take him just the way he is," Coach McKillop replied with a dismissing smile and confidence.

Sonya was overjoyed that someone finally saw her son as being good enough, just the way he was.

The fall of 2006, Sonya Curry kissed her son goodbye and watched him drive off to enter his freshman year at Davidson College. Knowing that the school's campus and John M. Belk Arena were only a half an hour drive from Charlotte kept her from worrying—as much.

The 2006–07 season at Davidson was when Stephen really began to make a mark in the basketball world. He would lead the Wildcats to a 29–5 record, a Southern Conference title, and the NCAA Tournament. He also set the NCAA record for most three-pointers made in a season by a freshman with 122. He led the Southern Conference in scoring with an average of 21.5 points per game. Only one college freshmen scored more than Curry, the University of

Texas's single-season star, Kevin Durant.

Stephen's deadly scoring ability and boyish appearance earned him the nickname "the Baby-Faced Assassin." However, the record-breaking freshman year that earned him the nickname didn't get off on the best start.

The first game of the season against Eastern Michigan, many people were waiting to watch Steph Curry play. Stephen lost the ball at tip-off over and

> *For years, Curry had practiced shots from such a distance that it would only be acceptable to shoot in a 'buzzer beater' end-of-game scenarios. McKillop knew Curry's range and told him he had the green light to shoot from anywhere on the floor. That confidence was all Stephen needed.*

over. At one point, he threw a pass straight into the crowd assuming his teammate was cutting to the hoop when he wasn't. Stephen had a whopping nine turnovers before half time. Most players would be benched after four, but Coach Bob refused to take him out.

Just before the start of the season McKillop had been talking to former Davidson Wildcats at an alumni event, "I told them that we had this freshman that was going to be a program-changer," the Davidson coach said. "Wait till you see Steph Curry. He is something special." The alumni who had heard this surely thought the coach had gone mad after seeing that first half 'glimpse.'

Fortunately, there was another half to play and Bob McKillop knew Stephen better than Stephen knew himself. With only two minutes and thirty-five seconds remaining in the game, McKillop's faith was rewarded. Stephen hit a quick three pointer, giving Davidson a one-point lead and then another to increase the lead by four. Eastern Michigan unable to recover went on to lose the game, 81–77. Stephen had self-corrected his own mistakes before coming back from halftime.

McKillop knew he was a fast learner on and off the court. After showing up to his first practice several minutes late, he was kicked out. "I told him he had to find another place to practice because he wasn't practicing with us that day," Coach Bob

College recruiters and scouts took one look at Stephen -his boyish face, thin frame- and either walked the other way or thought to themselves that there was just no way, he couldn't play at that level. Coach Bob McKillop was able to see in Stephen what all others could not.

remembered. "Steph never was late again."

In only his second game against the University of Michigan, Steph had thirty-two points, nine rebounds, and four assists. The team lost three of their first seven games. After that, the Wildcats went on a run, losing only one game of the next twenty-three. McKillop had been right about Curry, he was program-changer for Davidson. The year prior, the Wildcats finished 10–5 in conference play. They improved to 17–1 with the addition of the Baby-Faced Assassin. Davidson had earned a thirteenth seed in the 2007 NCAA Tournament and would face-off against fourth seeded Maryland in the first round.

"March Madness" begins after the regular season ends, with nearly all its games being played in the month of March, hence the first word of NCAA Tournament's nickname. The second word, Madness, refers to the frequent and unpredictable upsets during a tournament.

Stephen scored thirty points in the televised 82–70 loss to Maryland, but many were impressed watching the guard play for the first time.

CHAPTER FOUR

The Cinderella Season

The first eight games of the Wildcats' schedule in 2007 featured powerhouse programs including the North Carolina Tar Heels, Duke Blue Devils, and UCLA Bruins. All teams were ranked in the top ten, with Davidson's second game facing the Tar Heels, who only trailed Kansas in the polls.

Curry hit five three-pointers, finishing with twenty-seven points in Davidson's home opener at Belk Arena. Then dropped twenty-four points during a game in Chapel Hill against Michael Jordan's alma mater, only losing the game by five thanks to a late game comeback. After the game, Tar Heels head coach Roy Williams admitted he made a mistake on Curry, "Curry would be a good player regardless of what league he's in. He has a chance to play basketball for a living. He's a kid where [teams]—the University of North Carolina included—can say, 'Hey, we missed that kid.'"

The Assassin came out for the Southern Conference opener, connecting on nine shots from behind the arc against Appalachian State to finish with thirty-eight points, outscoring the combined efforts of all other Davidson players. They then struggled, shooting against seventh-ranked Duke. However they only lost by six thanks to twenty

During the 2008 Tournament, #30 who everyone said wasn't good enough to play for them, dominated. Leading a school of less than 2,000 students over schools with 30,000+

points from Steph. "Two times we've been in this gym [Belk Arena] and we've been right there with them," Curry said after the 79–73 loss. The Goliath-fighting Wildcat program of Davidson would suffer one more loss to the UCLA Bruins, who went 35–4 on the season and featured future NBA stars Russell Westbrook and Kevin Love.

After the loss to UCLA, Davidson didn't lose again. In fact, they won the twenty-two remaining games on the Wildcats schedule, ending the year a perfect 20–0 in Southern Conference games. Davidson also finished the season ranked twenty-third in the country, which was shocking for any mid-major school. During Stephen's breakout sophomore season, he averaged 25.9 points a game (fourth best in the nation). The Baby-Faced Assassin set a new all-time NCAA record for most-three-pointers in a season with 162 (43.9 % three-point field goal percentage). He sunk nearly 90% of his shots from the free throw line for the season, in addition to averaging two steals, 2.9 assists, and 4.6 rebounds per game. He was named the Southern Conference Player-of-the-Year and voted second-team All-

American. As impressive as these accomplishments and awards were, it was what happened next that would turn Stephen Curry into a household name.

During March Madness of 2008, the tenth-seeded Wildcats faced off against seventh-seeded Gonzaga. The Zags were a run-and-gun team that could catch fire, hitting threes and attacking the lanes. Davidson had Stephen Curry who could also catch on fire.

Gonzaga led 41–36 at halftime. Stephen went into the locker room with ten points and came out the Baby-Faced Assassin loaded with thirty. He fired nine rounds from three-point land, hitting his target eight times. The Wildcats led by two with less than two minutes remaining. The Zags tied it up, seventy-four each. On next possession, the Wildcats missed a three-pointer then hurried back on defense, assuming a Zags rebound. Curry spotted teammate Andrew Lovedale come up with the rebound-turned-loose ball. Stephen sprinted back towards Lovedale, slowing before the three-point line. Lovedale quickly got Curry the ball, loading the deadly Davidson weapon. The clock showed 1:04 left and with the whole country watching, Dell Curry's son knocked down a three with such perfection that the net barely moved.

"This game, he showed the whole nation what he's capable of," said Stephen's teammate Davidson point guard Jason Richards, who led the nation in assists by just giving the ball to Steph. Curry's performance that night was just the start of what would become one of the greatest Cinderella runs in NCAA Tournament history.

Everyone knew Davidson couldn't match up against the second-seeded Hoyas, who had a history

With each nail-biting, come from behind win, stories about number thirty's performances spread through schools, offices, campuses, elevators and more and more tuned in the following week to see what Stephen Curry would do next.

of basketball greatness that produced superstars such as Patrick Ewing, Alonzo Mourning, and Allen Iverson. Davidson couldn't do much in their game against Georgetown, thanks to seven-foot, two-inch center Roy Hibbert and six-foot, nine-inch Patrick Ewing Jr., son of the legendary Knicks center by the same name. Things weren't looking good for the Wildcats at halftime. Their superstar only had five points, and they were down by eleven.

With under ten minutes in the second-round game left, Curry came alive. Almost as if he flipped an imaginary switch. With the Steph-switch flipped on, he hit a three, threatened another with a pump-fake, pulling Georgetown out of the paint, leaving a Curry teammate open. Two more points for Davidson, an assist for Curry. Repeat. The nitro-fueled play caught the Wildcats up to Georgetown. With the Steph-switch left in the on position, Curry scored thirteen more points in the final five minutes to win the game. The 74–70 upset of the number-two seed ranks as one of the biggest upsets in recent history. Coach McKillop was stunned.

"I'm numb right now," was all he could say after

the game. Davidson College was so proud of their team that they offered to pay for all of their students to attend Davidson's next game in the tournament.

On March 28, 2008 at Ford Field in Detroit, Michigan, third-seeded Wisconsin played Davidson. Whether those in attendance rooted for the Wildcats or the Badgers, they all came to see Stephen play. Even NBA superstar LeBron James came. "I'm here to watch the kid," the four-time MVP who sat a few rows behind Davidson's bench, said. Everyone came to see 'the kid' do the impossible. For weeks,

Stephen was humble, he never bragged about himself and people liked him even more. Every week, Davidson would face off against a new "Goliath" and he was the underdog that people related with and rooted for.

Curry's heroics were the talk of SportsCenter. His spectacular highlights frequently made the Top 10 section, which famously concluded the ESPN program. He became the topic of discussion in the sports world, his NBA future debated by coaches, former players, and basketball critics. So many loved to cheer for Stephen, but few had faith that his game was more than a stroke of luck.

Focused and ready to play against Wisconsin, Steph ripped off his tear-away warmups. The shortened Bible verse written in black on the red trim of his shoes was visible. "I can do all things," was a shortened version of Philippians 4:13 which reads "I can do all things through Christ who strengthens me."

He wrote "I can do all things" on his shoes, and he was proving to the world that he could.

He scored a game-high thirty-three points against Wisconsin, one of the country's best defensive teams. It was his third-straight Tournament game where he scored more than thirty points. At the end of the first half, the game was locked at 36–36. Curry outscored the Badgers all by himself in the second half. Stephen scored twenty-two, but Wisconsin scored only twenty. The Wildcats won 73–56 for their twenty-fifth straight win of the season.

"This guy is going to be unbelievable," said Green Bay Packers quarterback Aaron Rodgers, who had driven nearly eight hours to watch the game. Davidson and Curry had again done the impossible.

The University of Kansas, KU for short, was the number one team in college basketball that year. The Kansas program is considered one of the most successful and prestigious programs in the history of the game. James Naismith, who invented the sport by nailing fruit baskets to balcony railings on opposing sides of a gym to use for goals, was KU's first coach! As if Goliath needed to appear any taller for the Davidson Wildcats. They were facing the second-most winning team of all-time with a record thirty-seven-win season. The 2007–08 Jayhawks were scoring machines, beating opponents with an average of twenty-eight points per game at home!

The game was supposed to be a blowout, a Jayhawks highlight film at the least. It would be neither. Kansas led by five points with under a minute to go in the game. The KU team ran a four-guard rotation that never tired against Curry. Curry

Teammate Jason Richards referred to the 2008 season as "Steph Curry's coming-out party." He became a player worth watching.

managed to get the ball and fired a three-pointer a split-second after catching the ball. The Davidson crowd erupted with excitement after the ball splashed through the net. The Davidson Wildcats were within a basket of winning.

The Jayhawks backcourt poorly executed a stall, leaving 16.8 seconds on the clock for Davidson, who trailed by only two points, 57–59. Curry dribbled the ball across half court, towards a waiting screen at the top of key. Too much space was left, and his defender followed Steph right through. With only 2.9 seconds remaining and two defenders covering him, Steph prepared to shoot. He found and zipped ball to an unguarded Richards at the last second. Richards launched a deep three-pointer towards the basket. The buzzer sounded, and the crowd went crazy.

"We had all the confidence in the world that we could beat mighty Kansas, the number one seed," Stephen said. But they didn't. The last-second shot was off to the left and missed. The KU crowd went crazy. Kansas would go on to win the National Championship, having no other team in the tournament come as close to beating the Jayhawks as the Wildcats that year.

"That was a tough game," said Curry, who was picked Most Outstanding Player of the Midwest Regional. They weren't predicted to come within twenty points "It's bittersweet," added Curry.

Although Stephen's stat line was amazing (32 points per game, 4.25 rebounds per game, 4.25 assists per game, 3.25 steals per game), his fame wasn't from that. Stephen had proven himself a hero who, against all the odds, beat the big guys. He made believers out of people again and inspired many to look at challenges within their own lives differently.

Steph and Ayesha had always been interested in each other, but Ayesha's parents didn't allow her to date in high school.

Everyone wanted to talk to the hero. He was interviewed by ESPN and other various sports programs. Even non-sports shows wanted to talk to him, like Late Night with Conan O'Brien. Stephen had just been nominated for an ESPY award for Best Breakthrough Athlete. He flew to Los Angeles, California, where his childhood friend Ayesha lived, to accept the award. He first met Ayesha in Charlotte as a teenager in their church's youth group. Stephen was fifteen years old, and Ayesha was fourteen. They both were too shy to talk to the other. After finding out what Stephen's favorite candy was, Ayesha began looking for Steph after church. "I was so shy I didn't say anything. I just handed him the candy and walked off," laughed Ayesha, who attended Weddington High, a twenty-minute drive from Stephen's Charlotte Christian. She graduated high school a year early and moved to Los Angeles to pursue a career in acting. Years later, she would find a message from Stephen in her Facebook inbox.

"I didn't know what the ESPYs were," Ayesha laughed. The two had plenty of things in common, but a love for sports wasn't one of them. She wrote

Stephen back, and the two set up a date, but both would've turned red at the time had the other called it that.

"She really didn't know what I did at the time," Stephen remembered, referring to his legendary

The two first 'kind of' met as teenagers at a Church youth group in Charlotte, but they were too shy to talk to each other so Ayesha would give him his favorite candy then run off. "That's how she would flirt with him... find him after church, barely say two words, and walk away..." Steph's younger sister, Sydel, was annoyed by her but knew Stephen liked it!

2008 Tournament performance. "It was pretty refreshing."

Ayesha picked Stephen up in her old van, and the two spent the day together walking around shops, taking pictures, and joking and laughing together.

"He was so funny and silly," Ayesha remembered. From that day on, the two spent as much time together as they could.

It was almost time for school to start back up again, and although Stephen could have entered the NBA draft, he chose to return to Davidson for his junior year. Coach McKillop and Stephen strategically agreed to switch him to the point guard position for the year. The two were considering his future in the NBA. At six feet, three inches, he would be an undersized NBA shooting guard, but would fit right in at the point position.

Stephen had a spectacular year, leading the nation in scoring with an average of 28.6 points per game. He was selected first team All-American, voted Southern Conference Player of the Year, and was a Wooden Award finalist. His per-game averages were even better than the year before: 28.6 points per game, 4.4 rebounds per game, 5.6 assists per game, 2.5 steals per game. The Wildcats finished 27–8, nearly making the NCAA Tournament a third straight year.

It would've been a great season for any other mid-major program, but it was average at best for all the Wildcat players, coaching staff, and fans who were a part of the magical 2007–08 season the year before. It was time for the school's all-time leading scorer and forever hero Stephen Curry to part ways with Davidson College and their inspiring coach, who always believed in him and what he could become.

CHAPTER FIVE

The Rookie

Although considered a top-ten pick, many teams were concerned with Curry's 'lack of athleticism.' It was the same "not big enough, not good enough" song that Stephen had heard his whole life.

"He was great in college, but he won't make it in the NBA," said draft analyst Scott Schroeder.

"He probably is never going to end up being a star in the league because of a lack of explosiveness," said *Bleacher Report*.

Scouting reports from NBAdraft.net would include that Stephen was "Far below NBA standard" and that he "needs to add some muscles to his upper body but [it] appears as though he'll always be skinny."

A pre-draft scouting report, provided by a former NBA head coach, listed Curry's perceived weaknesses as: "Shot-selection, unable to defend NBA guards, relies too heavily on outside shot, frail frame, lacks quickness." The scout that evaluated Curry also advised his team not to select the Davidson College guard in the Draft because he "has limited upside," meaning he could never become anything more than average.

Draft day was held at WaMu Theatre inside Madison Square Garden, where the New York Knicks played. The Knicks' head coach Pat Riley had been interested in Curry since first watching him play. Like Coach McKillop, Riley saw more in Curry than just his shooting range. The three-time NBA coach of the year knew how to win and held five NBA titles. "The reason I really liked him was that he never backed down," said the Knicks coach, hoping Stephen wouldn't be selected before New York's eighth pick.

On June 29, 2009 Ayesha and the Curry family joined Stephen in New York, waiting patiently in the green room. There were no surprises after the first few selections were made. Oklahoma's Blake Griffin was the number one pick in the draft, chosen by the Los Angeles Clippers. The Memphis Grizzlies took the University of Connecticut's seven-foot, three-inch Hasheem Thabeet with the second pick.

Arizona State University's playmaker James Harden went third to the Oklahoma City Thunder, followed by Tyreke Evans to the Sacramento Kings.

Thanks to pre-draft trades, the Minnesota Timberwolves had both the fifth and sixth picks and were looking for a point guard in a draft with many players of that position. First, they chose

> *Of all the players chosen before Curry in the draft, only James Harden has achieved even close to the same amount of success.*

the international star Ricky Rubio, who began his professional career in Spain when he was only thirteen! Wanting to be sure they found their future floor general that year, the T-wolves grabbed another point guard, selecting Syracuse sophomore Jonny Flynn with the sixth pick. Stephen had one more pick to get through before it would be New York's turn.

Curry's agent Jeff Austin recalled the moment: "Once we got to the seventh, we were like, 'C'mon, don't pick him.'"

NBA commissioner David Stern stepped up to the podium in New York, announcing the next selection, "With the seventh pick in the 2009 NBA draft, the Golden State Warriors select Stephen Curry from Davidson College." There was a surround sound of boos from Knicks fans in attendance. This wasn't at all what Stephen, Ayesha, or Stephen's family was hoping for, but Steph just smiled, put on a Warriors baseball hat and headed to the stage to meet his new team. He wasn't being fake, he was just the type of guy that always takes the higher road.

Stephen responded the same when hearing that the Warriors' star guard Monta Ellis wasn't happy with the addition of Curry to the roster or the idea of the two playing together.

During an interview Ellis stated, "That won't work. Period." Ellis averaged twenty points per game for Golden State. "I just want to win. . . . We're not going to win that way," added Ellis.

It was a known fact that Monta wanted to be the Warriors' only playmaker. It was a rocky start for the rookie from Charlotte. Not only was he having to

Ayesha always loved to cook – taught Stephen how to cook and would be of no surprise that she would later open her own restaurant. Ayesha is the owner of 'International Smoke,' which currently has several locations throughout the U.S.

move away from his family and Ayesha, he had to move to a new city to play on a team where one of his teammates didn't want him.

Stephen started at point guard for the Warriors'  home opener against the Rockets on October 28, 2009. Finally, the moment he had been waiting for, the announcer he had heard only in his imagination as a boy was finally real. With the lights off in Oracle Arena, Stephen waited in his Warriors warmups until the announcer began, "In his first NBA season, from Davidson College, number thirty, Stephen

Curry was almost Rookie of the Year, but instead came in just behind draft-mate Tyreke Evans.

Curry!" The boy that everyone considered too small, too short, and not good enough had done it! Stephen made his dream come true.

In the Warriors' first possession of the game, Stephen tallied his first NBA assist off of a pick-and-roll, finding an open teammate under the hoop. A few minutes later, he dribbled to his right, running his defender right into a waiting screen, then crossed over heading to his left, pulling up for a jumper near the free throw line. Nothing but net: Stephen's first NBA points.

It wasn't long into his rookie season that teams starting using their guards to try and post-up Curry. Opposing teams' coaches, always looking for an advantage, assumed Stephen was an easy target because of his size. "I was, quote-unquote, a mismatch [appearing weaker than their guards]. But CJ [Young] had already been doing that to me for years. It's crazy the confidence I drew from that going into the league," Stephen would say, acknowledging that the challenges he faced in junior high had turned to his benefit as an adult.

Although it had been a rough season for the 26–

56 Warriors, finishing third to last in the Western Conference, it had been an excellent rookie season for the likeable point guard out of Davidson. He nearly led the NBA in steals, coming in second with 152 on the season. He was named to the All-Rookie first team and had great first-year statistics: 17.5 points, 1.9 steals, 5.9 assists, 4.5 rebounds, and 3.4 three-pointers (43.7% 3FG).

Stephen's best game would come in the final game of the Warriors season against the Trailblazers, where he scored forty-two points and had nine rebounds and eight assists, leading the Warriors to a 122–116 win in Portland.

The Warriors appeared to be a completely different team from the one before, but lost nearly the same amount of games. They had new jerseys designed, a new logo created, were under new owners, and would even start with a new coach. They announced that Mark Jackson would become head coach of the Warriors. Stephen was overjoyed with the news. His soon-to-be coach was his dad's former Toronto Raptors teammate who had frequently challenged then-twelve-year-old Stephen to shooting contests!

Stephen was the recipient of the league's Sportsmanship Award that season, an award voted on by players. Although he averaged almost nineteen points and six assists per game, it had been a particularly rough year for Stephen, suffering multiple ankle injuries. He oftentimes played through pain, only missing eight games in the year, but Stephen had torn ligaments in his ankle that required surgery.

The couple remain extremely close and are described as 'perfect for one another' in that they are both kind of dorky/funny and 100% genuine. They even have matching tatoo's

Tension in the NBA was rising with player's agents and team owners arguing over contracts and money. Stephen's contract was up soon and needed to be discussed, but the Warriors' star was focused on something else.

On the way home from one of Stephen's little sister Sydel's volleyball games, Stephen and Ayesha stopped at his parents' house to grab a board game. When they were walking up the driveway, Stephen stopped and asked Ayesha if she knew where they were standing. It was the same place where the couple had their first kiss.

"He pulled me close and started saying all these sweet things and then dropped down on one knee. I was in a state of shock," Ayesha said, remembering the moment that Stephen asked her to marry him.

"I knew I had found the right woman and I wanted to start a life with her. . . .She looked at the ring and asked if it was real," Stephen laughed. "The next thing I knew, people were screaming from inside the house. All of our family was inside waiting, it was awesome!"

Stephen was twenty-three and Ayesha was twenty-two when they were married on July 30, 2011.

CHAPTER SIX

Breaking Ankles Comeback

If there ever was a time in Stephen's career to extend the off-season with an NBA lockout, it was now. He was still recovering from surgery and could really use the extra time to strengthen his ankle. Stephen and Ayesha could use the extra time to get ready for the baby on the way. Stephen would soon be a father!

Meanwhile, the Golden State Warriors selected Washington State University shooting guard Klay Thompson with the eleventh overall pick in the 2011 NBA Draft. Klay's dad was a former NBA player, his mom played volleyball, and Klay had just set tournament records for scoring and three-point shooting. This sounded very familiar.

The lockout ended a few months after Stephen and Ayesha's first daughter Riley was born. The regular season games kicked off on Christmas Day.

During the Warriors' final 2011–12 preseason game, Stephen reinjured his right ankle. He recovered but wasn't well for long. Shortly thereafter, in a game against the Los Angeles Clippers, he injured his ankle once again.

"He was turning his ankle in completely nontraditional, crazy ways," remembered the Warriors' general manager Bob Myers. Three out of five games at the beginning of the 2011 season, Stephen would be forced to leave the game due to ankle injuries. Even with his ankles taped and the best braces worn, the vicious cycle continued to repeat itself.

"I'd never seen someone sprain his ankle like that prior to Steph. And I haven't seen it since," added Myers. Stephen would watch forty-four games from the bench that year as Golden State sunk lower in the standings. As hard as he tried to stay positive, he felt hopeless.

He had worked so hard to make it to the NBA, to hear his last name in introductions and to play a game he loved as a job. "I feel like I'm never going to be able to play again." His dream felt like it was slipping away.

Months went by, and Stephen, with a clean bill of health, laced up for the 2012–13 season with high hopes of staying healthy. The Warriors banked on this as well, offering a four-year, $44-million contract extension to Curry. Stephen did have a few minor ankle tweaks throughout the season, but not enough to derail his restored confidence. That was all he needed to finally play his game.

With Curry and fellow sharpshooter Klay Thompson sharing the backcourt, the Warriors were quickly becoming the NBA's best three-point shooting team. The duo had been given the

Riley Curry was born to shine! Her bubbly personality in interviews during the 2016 NBA Playoffs made her famous.

nickname the "Splash Brothers." It was a name given by a Warriors content producer, inspired by a Bay Area baseball duo in the nineties that fans called the "Bash Brothers." The term referred to Major League Baseball's Oakland Athletics' power hitters Jose Canseco and Mark McGwire. The two players could hit further than other players in their time just as the "Splash Brothers" could hit three-pointers from further out than other players on the court. Curry and Thompson had the ability to erase even the largest of point deficits in a matter of minutes. Thanks to numerous air strikes by Steph and Klay, the team was headed to the playoffs for the first time since the 2006–07 season.

Golden State was the sixth seed in the Western Conference facing off against the Denver Nuggets, who were a third. Splash Brothers shooting streaks became a regular occurrence during games, as did their highlights on SportsCenter. The Warriors breezed through Denver and into the second round to be met by the more experienced and very talented San Antonio Spurs, led by four-time NBA Champion Tim Duncan. Typically, teams hit by an arsenal of three-point bombs from Curry and Thompson are unable to recover and would naturally roll over. The Spurs were different, they came back. The consistent play of Duncan and guard Tony Parker led to a series win, eliminating the Warriors in six games.

During the playoffs, Warrior coach Mark Jackson gave the duo the ultimate compliment, calling the two "the greatest shooting backcourt in the history

Stephen Curry and Klay Thompson, both sons of former NBA players, both considered among the greatest shooters in league history, and one of the best backcourts (guards) of all time.

Stephen achieved his current career-high single-game scoring record on his first visit to the famous Madison Square Garden.

of the game."

An early pinnacle in Steph's career came on February 27, 2013. His performance against the Knicks that day had sports writers, analysts, and commentators crediting it as the start to Curry changing the game of basketball, forever.

It started the way every game at Madison Square Garden had, with four players from each team spread around center court where two waited to jump. The Golden State point guard had again written on his Nikes, "I can do all things," Stephen's favorite Bible verse.

The game had a pretty boring start, especially for Curry who, even several minutes into the second quarter, only had four points. He hit a jumper, a free-throw, then back-to-back three-pointers. He was starting to heat up.

He soon finds himself leading a three-on-two fast-break. The game situation was so frequent that the name also refers to the drill practiced at all levels since the game's creation. Coaches instruct players to fill three lanes on fast-break. A pass is made when the ball is stopped by defender for, almost always, a sure two points.

Curry was a few steps inside half court when he

begins to slow down. Those familiar with the game were thinking, "Time isn't expiring. A defender hasn't stopped you. What are you doing?" Swish, nothing but net. Curry knocks down a three. The game's knowledgeable elite didn't get it. Why risk a three, when you can get a sure two?

The spectacular and extremely ballsy play that would lead to any other player at any level to be benched was soon forgotten, distracted by Curry's next incredible play. His play on the court was hypnotizing. Going into halftime, the Baby-Faced Assassin had scored twenty-three points.

After half-time, he picked up right where he left off. Knicks defenders looked at their coaching staff as if to say, "How am I supposed to stop a guy that wants to shoot from thirty feet away?"

Then the moment showed itself again. Curry was leading another three-on-two. This time just inside half-court, Stephen slowed his dribble. The ball sailed through the air and Madison Square Garden stood still. The net barely moved. No one before Curry would dare break one of basketball's oldest laws, but even the old timers now understood. Why settle for two when you can surely get three?

"The mood in the arena was different. It's not just like, 'This guy's hot right now.' It's like, 'Something big is happening,'" remembers Warrior forward Harrison Barnes.

He hit a franchise record eleven three-pointers that night on his way to fifty-four points. That wasn't the amazing thing, though. ESPN analyst Doris Burke possibly said it best, "It never crossed my mind that this individual would basically change the definition of what is and is not a quality shot in the NBA."

Stephen was the only person to score above 50 points in one game with ten or more three-pointers.

CHAPTER SEVEN

The Rise of a Star

As Steph's influence grew, so did his popularity, providing more opportunities to help others. His charity Nothing-But-Nets handed out nearly forty thousand bed nets during the off season to fight Malaria in Tanzania. Steph partnered with the Make-A-Wish foundation, frequently visiting young children battling serious illnesses. During Christmas, he and Ayesha bought food for hundreds of families in the Bay Area.

"There is no better feeling than doing something for others," Stephen said.

Stephen hoped to re-sign a shoe deal with Nike, but the company put little effort or value in the three-point marksman. Then he was approached by Under Armour, an athletic outfitting company that was hardly known in the basketball industry at the time.

They believed in Steph's market value and his future. Soon, the two inked a deal and created Stephen's custom shoe that included his initials. This later became his logo and included his number '30.'

Under Armour's timing to sign Stephen couldn't have been better. A month later, in December, Curry set the Warrior franchise record for most career three-pointers while he was wearing UA's custom shoe. In January, he was one of NBA's top vote-getters for the 2014 NBA All-Star Game. In February,

When it was time to resign with Nike, Dell and Stephen flew out and listened to a Nike salesman prounounce Stephen's name as Steff–in the entire time. This wasn't a big deal to Steph, neither was the money, but what was a big deal was having a basketball camp put on by the company like one he used to attend as a kid. Nike declined. Steph signed with Under Armour and is said to be worth over $14 Billion to the company.

he stepped onto the court sporting his popular UA kicks for the league's sixty-third annual All-Star game and the first NBA All-Star weekend of his career. This level of consistent exposure from an idolized player translated into millions of dollars in increased revenue for a company. UA's decision to pursue the NBA's fastest-rising star proved to be brilliant.

Curry had rained 261 three-pointers during the 2013–14 season, tops in the NBA that year, and good for third-most all-time. He upped his per-game averages in points (24.0 per game), assists (8.5 APG), and rebounds (4.4 RPG). Stephen received a huge league honor by being named second team All-NBA.

Golden State had officially turned the ship around, finishing the regular season with a 51–31 record and making the playoffs for a second consecutive year. The sixth-seeded Warriors drew the Los Angeles Clippers and would face Blake Griffin and the team nicknamed Lob City in the first round. The name referred to the team's above-the-rim style of play. Frequently lobs or alley-oops were thrown near the rim and Griffin or DeAndre Jordan would grab them mid-air to slam into the hoop.

The series was a back and forth battle with every game being entirely different than the ones before it. The Warriors forced a tie-breaking Game Seven to decide the series. They had edged out Los Angeles by one point two nights earlier. It was a rough series for the Splash Brothers. The Clippers' defense frequently double-teamed the duo, forcing Curry to find other ways for Golden State to score.

Ultimately, Griffin and Jordan proved to be too much for the Warriors to handle, and the Clippers

After leaving the Warriors, Jackson returned to his previous job as a broadcast commentator and game analyst for ESPN.

won Game Seven, 126–121, which signaled the end of the Warriors season as Los Angeles advanced to the conference semifinals.

Stephen and other Warriors players stated publicly that they were upset with management's decision to fire coach Mark Jackson after the team's early exit from the playoffs. It was frustrating because they had become a tight-knit group and Coach Jackson created that. Bay Area's fan base, called Dub Nation, was concerned as well. The team then announced that former Bulls sharpshooter Steve Kerr would become the Warriors new head coach. Kerr had been a former point guard with the Chicago Bulls in the 1990s during the Michael Jordan era that won six NBA Championships.

The Warriors won their first five games of the2014 season. The players were happy, Kerr was happy, Dub Nation was happy, and the team owners were happy. Although many loved and missed the motivating Mark Jackson, the Bay Area began to realize that Steve Kerr's vision and strategy was needed to take the franchise to the next level.

Part of Kerr's strategy was installing a fast-paced

continuous-motion offense built around Curry. In previous years, Steph was forced to create his own shots off the dribble. The new strategy granted complete freedom to all of the players. A player could give up the ball, run off multiple screens set by teammates, then get the ball back to shoot, pass, or do it all again. To be effective, the offense only required two things: speed and constant ball movement.

Kerr coached his team based on player strengths. For example, had Draymond Green played on another

Led by Kerr, the Warriors broke the record for the most wins in a season. Kerr had helped set the record in 1995 when he played for the Chicago Bulls.

team, he most likely would have been assigned under the hoop on both sides of the court, a disadvantage based on the power forward's undersized six-foot, seven-inch frame. However, under Kerr's offense, Green could move around freely on offense, using his speed and outside shooting as an advantage, forcing opposing coaches to try and match up to the Warriors rather than other way around.

The perfect game to test Kerr's offense and lineup strategy was a rematch against the Clippers. With the same rosters and lineups, there would be few unknown variables. The results of the game were shocking. The team had the exact same players, but was a completely different team. The Clippers were never able to play their dominant game, they were too busy trying to keep up with Golden State's lightning-fast ball movement that never stopped. The Warriors won easily, 121–104.

CHAPTER EIGHT

The Kerr Effect

The Warriors had best start in their sixty-nine-year franchise history and went 10–2 Between mid-November and mid-December, the team had another franchise best with sixteen straight wins, improving the team's record to 21–2 for the first quarter of the season.

Stephen thrived under Kerr's direction and had officially become a superstar. "The guy has taken it to another level. I think he's the best in the NBA right now at the position," said Kerr about his point guard's play. His awesome coach also encouraged Steph to step up his defense as well to match his offense. This was something coaches before had never done. Kerr had confidence in Stephen and frequently gave him the task of guarding opposing teams' stars. Curry rewarded his coach by leading the entire NBA in steals.

The Splash Brothers were also in full effect. The team had become unstoppable behind their leader. The Baby-Faced Assassin was as clutch as they come. His late-game heroics inspired a new nickname thanks to well-known rapper Drake. Steph became

The player who nearly everyone said couldn't play Division I college basketball, had the best individual NBA season ever recorded.

Chef, and Chef Curry's end of game heroics were no longer reserved for game's end. The switch that turned regular Stephen into the Assassin or Chef had been stuck in the on position for basically the entire 2014–15 season.

Everyone on the Warriors seemed to be thriving in the new offense. On January 23, 2015, Klay Thompson didn't miss a shot in the entire third quarter against the Sacramento Kings, and he shot a lot. Many of his thirteen shots were from long-range. Klay held the new NBA record for most points scored in a quarter of basketball with thirty-seven!

A month later, Thompson would suit up for his first All-Star game. Stephen became the NBA's highest vote-getter for the 2015 NBA All-Star game, beating out LeBron James with 1.5 million votes.

The Splash Brothers would go on to set the record for most three-pointers made by teammates in a season with 525, breaking their own previous record of 484! Stephen would also pass himself in the record books for most threes by a player, with 286 for the year. Stephen earned ALL-NBA first-team honors for his play in the regular season. His per-game averages continued to rise with 23.8 points per game, 7.7 assists, 4.3 rebounds, and 2.0 steals. He led the NBA in free-throw percentage, steals, and nearly every three-point shooting category there was!

This Golden State squad would be considered one of the best ever, posting a franchise-record sixty-seven-win season. They advanced to a third straight post-season and clenched the top playoff spot. Much had changed from the underdog Warriors team that entered the first round three years before. The team also wasn't the same selfish squad with players who didn't like each other or their coaches. They were the opposite, very supportive, and each other's biggest fans. The super-hero-like team had emerged as a tight family of characters with Superhero Steph; his younger Splash Brother Klay; Draymond Green, who had become the perfect complement to the duo by doing the dirty work; and Coach Kerr, the mastermind.

In round one of the 2015 NBA Playoffs the superheroes faced the underdog New Orleans Pelicans. Golden State flew by them without a loss in four straight games.

Stephen and Ayesha had family in town for a few of the second-round games against the fifth-seeded Memphis Grizzlies. When Curry arrived home after the Game One, 101–86, win, he was greeted by "the cheesiest smiles you could ever imagine," remembered the star. He noticed they were all oddly wearing matching Under Armour shirts. Sydel looked at Steph and pointed to her shirt which read: 'SC 30 MVP'. It stood for Stephen Curry, his jersey number, and Most Valuable Player. He didn't believe it at first. It is the highest individual honor a basketball player can receive. It's given only once a year to the very best.

Daughters Riley and Ryan are their dad's biggest fans.

He was in shock. Later that night, he thought back to junior high. He was so small that he had no choice but to shoot as far away as possible. CJ Young had knocked him down so many times that it felt like he spent his whole childhood getting back up. Then Virginia Tech and every Division One school snubbed him. "That was horrible," he thought. He had to work twice as hard for NBA teams to even notice him at small Davidson College.

It all made sense. Stephen leaned back in his chair and tears began to roll down his cheeks and

> *Stephen proved to the world that someone with determination, passion and an unwillingness to ever give up is more important than size, strength, and athletic ability.*

To the Curry's, family always takes priority above basketball.

drip onto his shirt. It was in his times of struggle and pain that he grew the most.

The following day, Stephen was given the 2015 NBA Most Valuable Player trophy. He thanked those in his life who helped him along the way. His grandparents, his wife Ayesha, his parents, his coaches, and many others. Before the Oracle Center audience gave their applause, Stephen said:

"When it (came) to basketball, I was always the smallest kid on my team. I had a terrible, ugly shot from the time I was fourteen because I wasn't strong enough to shoot over my head. You'd think there are no hurdles or obstacles that I had to overcome, but even when I got to high school, I wasn't ranked. You don't have to live anybody else's story. It doesn't matter where you come from, what you have or don't have, what you lack, what you have too much of—all you need to have is faith in God, an undying passion for what you do or what you choose to do in this life, and a relentless drive and the will to do whatever it takes to be successful in whatever you put your mind to."

CHAPTER NINE

We are the Champions

The series win against the Grizzlies meant the Warriors were only four wins away from playing for an NBA Championship. Four wins against James Harden's Houston Rockets don't come easy. The game would be a battle between the guards, Curry versus Harden. Harden had been second behind Steph in MVP votes and was one of the fiercest guards in the league. Houston Rockets also had six-foot, eleven-inch center Dwight Howard, who was a freak of nature in terms of athletic gifts.

The Warriors barely edged out Houston in Game One, winning, 110–106. Curry scored thirty-four points himself.

All everyone could talk about was Curry's outrageous behavior at the press conference following Game One. Curry had crawled under a table, hid behind a curtain, and handed used chewing gum to a reporter! The Curry everyone was

Riley is always outspoken about her dad, even in his televised interviews!

talking about was Stephen's two-year-old daughter Riley Curry! As a room full of reporters listened to Steph talk about the Rockets game, Riley didn't want to hear it! "Daddy be quiet and get to work!" The adorable Riley said to her MVP father.

The Splash Brothers would secure a Warriors victory in the final seconds of Game Two. Harden brought up the ball with Houston trailing 98–99. He was met with a defensive trap set by Steph and Klay that would cause the star to lose the ball and preserve a win for Dub Nation.

Chef Curry served up forty points to Houston in Game Three. Harden answered with forty-five in Game Four. It all changed in Game Five with Steph putting up twenty-six points and Harden having one of his worst performances ever with twelve turnovers. The Warriors were headed to the NBA Finals for the first time in thirty years!

Golden State had officially become a powerhouse. For most of the season, they went unchallenged. Now they faced the Cleveland Cavaliers and the Big-Three: Kyrie Irving, Kevin Love, and LeBron James. However, the Warriors would face only two of the

Big Three. Kevin Love was out for the entire series. LeBron James had a combination of unreal talent and the heart to match, which created one of the greatest athletes to ever play the game. Not a single player on the Warriors' team had finals experience, yet they would be tasked with playing against a four-time MVP playing in his fifth consecutive finals.

The first two games went into overtime. Golden State won the first behind Stephen's twenty-six points despite James putting up forty-four points. In Game Two, Curry struggled with connecting from three-land, making only two of fifteen shots. Meanwhile, a monster triple-double from James with thirty-nine points, sixteen rebounds, and eleven assists tied the series at 1–1. The Cavs' point guard Kyrie Irving was taken out for the series because of an injury, and the Warriors got their break. They only had to face the Big One, LeBron James. Nearly the same production came from the one-man-show who, in Game Three, single handedly beat the Warriors with forty points to Steph's twenty-seven points.

Looking for an advantage while their backs were against the wall, Coach Kerr rearranged the lineup to include another versatile swingman, Andre Iguodala. Although the Warriors were unable to stop James, who averaged an incredible 35.8 points, 13.3 rebounds, and 8.8 assists in the series, they found a way to slow him. Iguodala deserved much of the credit, lowering the superstar's shooting percentage to 38.1%. Kerr's creativity proved to be all that was needed for the Warriors to do what they hadn't since 1975. They won the NBA Championship!

After the game, LeBron James found the league's newest NBA Champion and MVP to congratulate him. It had been seven years since LeBron had gone

Popping the champagne after the Championship win.

"to see the kid" who played for Davidson. The kid who had practiced alone for years and years to master a game he was told he couldn't play was now being rewarded for it. Holding his daughter Riley, Stephen stepped on stage to claim the O'Brien NBA Championship Trophy.

CHAPTER TEN

The Best Ever

Now everyone knew what Stephen Curry could do. Coaches watched him more, and defenders guarded him further out. Curry somehow got better, a lot better it turned out. His first game of the season, he had forty points; his third, fifty-three; his tenth, forty-six; and it continued like this. He scored forty points or more seven times while leading the Warriors to the best start in NBA history, going 24–0. By the time the 2015–16 regular season had ended, Curry effectively made it impossible for his critics, doubters, and haters to even open their mouth. He led the Warriors to the best-ever NBA regular-season. They went 73–9, surpassing what many had called one of the greatest seasons in sports history, Michael Jordan's 1995–96, 72-win Chicago Bulls team that Coach Kerr played on.

Stephen led the NBA in steals for a second straight year with 2.1 per game, scoring with a

30.1-point average, and free-throw accuracy with 90.8%. Perhaps most incredible was his forty-six percent accuracy shooting thirty feet or more away

Stephen has proven himself to be the best shooter the game of basketball has ever seen.

from the basket. Only Curry has ever shot from this distance regularly, as it literally is just a few big steps inside half court. Stephen absolutely shattered his already-impressive most-ever mark of 286 total three-pointers in a season with 402!

Ayesha and Stephen were again proud parents to an adorable daughter, Ryan Curry. Like a good big sister, Riley was ready to help her mom take care of Ryan. Within a few years, the two would be best friends and sometimes worst enemies. They were now the Curry family of four and were given the title of the NBA's First Family. The name referenced the name for the President of the United States, The First Family. Stephen was the president of the NBA.

"It was the greatest individual season in NBA history," said Fox Sports, among a million other networks, reporters, and fans. He not only was voted MVP of the league for a second time, he became the only unanimous MVP in NBA history. Every sports reporter filling out the five player spots on the MVP ballot that year had written Stephen Curry at the top of the list. Coach Kerr stood behind the podium and looked at his point guard in the front row.

"Winning the MVP last year wasn't enough. You came back this year dramatically better. That's amazing. How does that happen? It has to

Steph goes above and beyond not only for basketball but also for his family.

be something inside. . . . I think what makes you special, it's the determination, it's the love for the game," said the Golden State coach. "The other reason you won [the second MVP award] is your incredible confidence. I've seen very, very few players that possess the confidence that you have."

On February 27, 2016, Golden State faced Oklahoma City in a regular season battle that seemed to have a direct correlation to the 2016 Western Conference Finals between the two. The Thunder featured two of NBA's best with 2013–14 MVP Kevin Durant and the just-as-impressive triple-double artist, point guard Russell Westbrook. Oklahoma City got off to an early lead thanks to solid shooting by Durant. The Thunder led the Warriors, 30–20, at the end of the first quarter and the first game of the series two months later. Towards the end of the second quarter, in rapid succession that took less than a minute, Curry knocked down three straight three-pointers, erasing the lead.

The same would happen in Game Two behind twenty-eight points from Chef Curry to tie the series, 1–1. Stephen jumped in front of Westbrook to intercept a pass from Durant. At the other end of the court, he lifted off towards the hoop but dished the ball out for an assist before landing. Westbrook—who had leaped from behind Curry—came down directly on Curry's ankle. The momentum slammed the Warriors star to the ground and into the base of the hoop. Stephen struggled just to get up and was forced to leave the game. Curry did not return to the game until only minutes remained in the fourth quarter.

The Thunder led 3–1 in the Western Conference Finals, winning both Games Three and Four. The

Golden State Warriors: NBA Champions 2015, 2017, and 2018!

Warriors were one loss away from being eliminated. Behind back-to-back thirty-one-point games, Stephen helped Golden State get back up with two straight playoff wins that tied the best-of-seven series, 3–3.

Down by nine points with only 3:37 left in the final game, Curry knocked in a bundle of three-pointers to help tie the game, 103–103. The game headed to overtime.

Oklahoma City jumped ahead 108–103 within the first thirty seconds in the five-minute long overtime. Stephen scored nine points to keep pace with the Thunder, 118–118. With ten seconds left, Westbrook pulled up, shooting the game-winner. It bounces off, the Warriors rebound, and outlet to Curry.

What was supposed to happen: Stephen would cross half-court, call a timeout, and the Warriors would draw up a last-second play to get off a good shot.

What actually happened: Stephen crossed half court with 3.3 seconds on the clock and calmly set up to shoot. He was thirty-six or thirty-seven feet away. It wasn't some heave from the side, nor did it appear to be any different from the free-throws he had shot just a minute earlier. It was all one smooth motion through his release.

As Curry dribbled across half court, going half-speed, the commentator for the game Mike Breen narrated "They do have a time-out." He was surprised as Stephen pulled up to shoot. Breen quickly rushing out words, "but decide not to use it" and paused as Curry's shot floated through the air.

"BANG! BANG! OH, WHAT A SHOT FROM CURRY!" Warriors won, 121–118.

People watching Stephen for the first time assumed it was luck, an end of game hail-Mary.

"Success is born out of faith, an undying passion, and a relentless drive."

Those who played against him, like Westbrook that night, still believe the shot was impossible.

"Everybody in this locker room, we've seen him practice from that range every day," Thompson said about his Splash Brother's game-winning three-pointer. It was his twelfth in the game and would tie an NBA record. It certainly wasn't luck, as these bombs are not one-time occurrences.

"You don't just learn to shoot like that on a whim," Stephen would say about his incredible shooting range that he'd been expanding since a boy. "I've shot the shot plenty of times. You're coming across half court and timing up your dribbles." It was practice and more practice. A relentless work ethic that constantly pushed him to take a step back on the court after everyone had gone home and shoot another from thirty-five feet. Curry had this consistent commitment since he was a boy, taking that same step back in the mud to shoot from twelve feet on Grandpa Jack's ugly hoop. As soon as it was mastered, he'd step back again. He pushed himself so far past the limit of other players that, when they would see him hit a thirty-five-foot shot, they assumed it was luck.

CHAPTER ELEVEN

The (NBA's) First Family

With the unanimous MVP selection that followed Curry's record-breaking 2015–16 season, Stephen's popularity and influence rapidly grew. Film companies wanted to make documentaries about him, others pitched a reality show starring him and Ayesha, then just Ayesha! A life-size dollhouse was built for Riley in their backyard for TLC's Playhouse Masters. Companies wanted Stephen to be their spokesperson or endorse their products, especially after reading about what he did for Under Armour. Since the two partnered, "UA's US basketball shoe sales have increased over 350%." Within just a few years, the company's basketball division had more than tripled in size.

Talk shows wanted him on as their guest. Reporters wanted to interview him. Schools, hospitals, and charities all wanted him to make an appearance. Stephen was asked to be in music videos, was pulled up on stage during music concerts, and even led a boxer's entourage out for his championship fight. The Carolina Panthers NFL team announced Stephen as an honorary member of the team and gave him an authentic jersey with

The success Stephen has had on the court, has led to many opportunities including starting his own film company, Unanimous Media, which focuses on strategically producing content on sports, family and faith.

"Curry" on the back. Everyone liked Stephen because of how down-to-earth and normal he was, despite being so famous. The President of the United States even wanted to hang out with Steph! President Barack Obama, Steph, and Steph's father Dell all went golfing!

He had reached the level of superstar status that only LeBron James has seen and that Michael Jordan had created. Stephen's star power may not be as widespread as James or Jordan, but his is unique. Six-foot, six-inch Michael and six-foot, eight-inch LeBron had measured verticals of forty-eight inches and forty inches, respectively, and could literally jump over defenders. Stephen had to solely depend on skills that can only be acquired through practice. Because of this, 'normal, everyday people' could relate with Stephen in a way they couldn't with James or Jordan. Like them, Curry was an underdog. He was beloved by fans from the beginning when they first cheered for "the kid" during his courageous Davidson versus Goliath takedowns of the powerhouse programs who hadn't recruited him.

Stephen is the type of guy who remembers to

thank the assistant equipment manager during an NBA MVP speech. Despite his fame, he has remained himself, humble and kind to others. The Warriors' general manager Bob Myers said to Stephen during the star's first MVP ceremony, "I know you're loved by a lot of people that don't know you, but the ones that know you, love you the most. That's a true testament to the type of person you are.

While playing for the Warriors, Durant reached 20,000 career-points, making him one of the top-fifty scorers in NBA history.

It was humbling for the Warriors to say the least. Despite posting the best record in NBA history and having a two-game lead in the Finals, the Warriors lost. The Cleveland Cavaliers won the next three games and the 2016 NBA Championship.

The loss was disappointing to all Warrior fans, employees in the organization, and the team. Their owner was willing to pay for it not to happen again. Oklahoma City's contract with superstar Kevin Durant was about to expire. Warrior owner Joe Lacob wanted Durant to play for the team and set up a meeting with the star. Typically, these meetings only include the player, his agent, and a few team executives. Joe Lacob thought it would be best if Kevin Durant heard from the Warriors' players and Coach Kerr, so he invited them to the meeting too! Curry told the talented forward that he "could care less who the star was, who scored the most, or who sold more shoes." Stephen then talked about how he and his teammates cared for one another and were each other's biggest fans.

"If you won the MVP award, I'd be in the front row clapping for you," added Steph to illustrate his point.

It wasn't long before the six-time NBA All-Star and four-time scoring leader joined the Warriors. Fans began using the term "the fantastic-four," referring

What started out as a player nobody thought could do anything, play on a team that no one wanted to watch, it is amazing to see all that has been accomplished.

to Durant, the Splash Brothers, and Draymond Green, all NBA All-Stars. The Warriors broke twenty records on the way to a 67–15 season, an identical record to their 2014–15 season, which was second-best in franchise history. Green was named the NBA Defensive Player of the Year along with being selected to the All-NBA third-team, joining Durant and Curry,

Canon Curry - born in 2018! Steph and Ayesha considered naming the new baby "Wardell Stephen Curry III" to continue the family tradition, but decided to use a unique name instead.

who made the second-team. The biggest difference with Durant on the team was their play during the postseason. They finished as World Champions after an incredible 16–1 playoff record that included three straight series-sweeps, losing only Game Three to Cleveland in the NBA Finals. Kevin Durant would win the award for NBA Finals MVP.

The following 2017–18 season produced nearly identical results with Golden State's second straight NBA Championship. Kevin Durant was named NBA Finals MVP for a second straight time.

That season also marked for the second straight time that Stephen stood in the front row clapping as Kevin Durant was presented the trophy for NBA Finals MVP.

Anthony Curcio is a five-time best-selling author. He has bachelor's degree in social sciences from Washington State University and is an educational consultant and speaker. He works with children and gives presentations regarding drug abuse prevention and the importance of making positive choices.

"I'm not the guy who's afraid of failure. I like to take risks, take the big shot and all that." – *Curry when questioned about fear.*

"Success is born out of faith, an undying passion, and a relentless drive." – *Curry Comment.*

"I was always the smallest kid on my team. I had a terrible, ugly, shot from the time I was 14 because I wasn't strong enough to shoot over my head. You'd think there are no hurdles or obstacles that I had to overcome, but even when I got to high school I wasn't ranked." – *Curry talking about his journey.*

"Find what you're passionate about in this life and just work at it." – *Curry about finding greatness.*

"It doesn't matter where you come from, what you have or don't have, what you lack or what you have too much of, but all you need to have is faith in God, an undying passion for what you do, and a relentless drive and the will to do whatever it takes." – *Curry during MVP acceptance speech.*

"Success comes after you conquer your biggest obstacles and hurdles." – *Curry when speaking about getting through injuries.*

"I hope I inspire people all around the world to just be themselves. Be humble and be grateful for all the blessings in your life." – *Curry when asked about how he wants to be remembered.*

1-on-1: When two players play against each other in a game.

3-on-2: refers to a game situation where three offensive players attempt to score against two defenders. Usually in fast-break situations.

Alley-oop: A pass thrown near rim for teammate to catch and slam or tip into the basket. Also called a 'lob.'

APG: Assists per game (abbreviation usually used with game statistics).

AP Poll: The Associated Press Poll gives weekly rankings of the top 25 NCAA teams in Division I college sports

Assist: A statistic that occurs when a player passes the ball to someone who scores after receiving the pass. The passing player is then credited with an assist on stat sheet.

Bay Area: Refers to area surrounding the San Francisco Bay including Oakland, San Jose and San Francisco.

Bench Player: players that are not in the starting lineup who can be substituted into the game

Bracket: a tree diagram that fans use to predict the winner of a tournament

Brick: Missed shot.

Chapel Hill: city where the University of North Carolina campus is in, connected to 'Tobacco Road' linking long-time rival and basketball powerhouse Duke University, located only 8 miles away.

Chemistry: Usually refers to a very positive, sometimes unique relationship with two or more players, often an entire team.

Clutch: When a players shooting accuracy is dependable, usually when referring to end of quarter or game.

Crossover: A dribble move used to quickly change direction.

Double-Team: Having two defensive players guarding one offensive player.

Fast-break: When a two or more offensive players try to score before majority of defenders catch up.

Goliath: a Giant, or powerhouse player or team that has significant advantage.

Lanes: Imaginary paths for players to move down. Typically used when referring to open court or fast break situations.

Lob: A pass thrown near rim for teammate to catch and slam or tip into the basket. Also called an 'alley-oop.'

Key: the area under the baskets market by lines on the court; also referred to as "the paint" or "the lane"

Layup: A shot taken from very close to the hoop. Usually shot on the move and performed with one hand.

Man-to-man: A type of defense played where one defender tasked with guarding one player and not an area on the court, like a zone.

MVP: Most Valuable Player; the title reserved for the best performing player in a particular game or series of games

One-and-done: An athlete who only plays one year of college sports, then enters professional draft.

Paint: The painted area that makes up the free throw lane.

Pick and Roll: a play in which an offensive player blocks the defender to free his teammate for the ball, and then moves towards the basket to receive a pass

Point Guard: player that dribbles up court to set up initial offensive play during each possession. Usually best ball handler and passer. Point guard objective is usually to distribute the ball to teammates to setup scoring opportunities.

Post: Two areas near the basket just outside of the key that are marked with two painted boxes. Also referred to as the block.

Post Up: Offensive move, where a player gets the ball in the post area/at the block, with his or her back to the basket.

Press: a defensive strategy where the defenders guard the opposing team closely the full (or sometimes half) length of the court.

Power Forward: typically, one of the tallest players who is responsible for blocking shots and grabbing rebounds.

PPG: Points per game (abbreviation usually used with game statistics).

Pump-fake: a fake shot.

RPG: Rebounds per game (abbreviation usually used with game statistics).

Run and Gun: a fast style of play/offense.

Shot Clock: a countdown to when the ball must leave the offensive team's hands and hit the rim before time expires, which results in turnover.

Slam: When a player puts ball through basket, touching rim with hands. Typically done forcefully. Also called 'slam-dunk.'

SPG: Steals per game (abbreviation usually used with game statistics).

Stall: An offensive strategy of slowing down the game, or control the clock in some ways. Usually done towards end of game when team is leading, or when attempting to shoot at a time.

Sweet 16: The name for the third-round games of the NCAA Tournament when only 16 teams remain.

Tip Off: the referee throws the ball up in air between two players of different teams to start the game. Identical to a 'jump ball,' except used only to start the game and preformed inside center circle.

Telegraphing: staring down the player that passer will throw to, which gives defender 'heads up' to make steal.

Upset: when a team expected to win is beat by an 'underdog' or a team not expected to win the game.

Wingspan: measured with arms and hands extended out from fingertip to fingertip

Zone: (a) When an individual player is having a hot shooting streak, with many consecutive shots made. Example: He hits another three, giving him 7 on the night, he really is in a zone right now.

(b) Type of defense. Rather than defender guarding a player, he or she is assigned to an area. Once a player enters that area, the defender would appear to be playing them man-to-man. Zone defense is not permitted in the NBA. Example: They're killing us man-to-man, switch to a 2-3 zone.

March 14, 1988: Curry born in Akron, Ohio

1993: Stephen stars in a Burger King commercial with his dad, Dell. It begins with Dell asking 6-year-old Stephen what he wants to be when he grows up. "A basketball player."

February, 2002: Stephen (and Seth) lead Queensway Christian College 7/8th grade basketball team to 16-0 season. Steph scores 44 points in championship game.

March, 2004: Stephen changes his shooting form prior to his junior season at Charlotte Christian High School He would lead the Knights to the state tournament and also earn all-conference and all-state honors.

February 1, 2006: Stephen signs to play at Davidson

March 21-30, 2008: Before the 2008 NCAA Tournament began, few knew of Stephen Curry. If they did, it was as Dell Curry's son. By the time it was over, everyone knew who the Davidson star was and Dell became known as Stephen Curry's dad!

June 25, 2009: Stephen is the 7th overall pick in the NBA draft by the Golden State Warriors

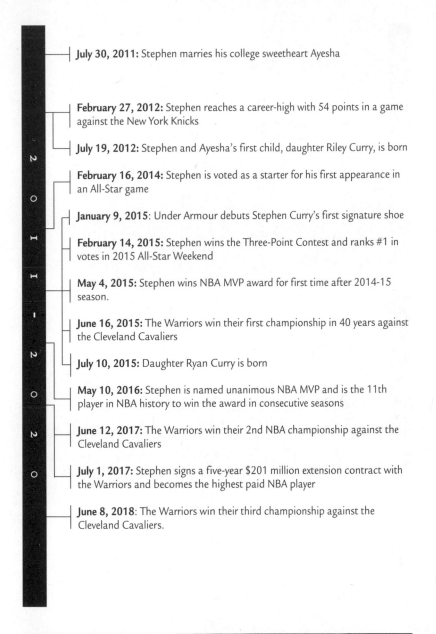

July 30, 2011: Stephen marries his college sweetheart Ayesha

February 27, 2012: Stephen reaches a career-high with 54 points in a game against the New York Knicks

July 19, 2012: Stephen and Ayesha's first child, daughter Riley Curry, is born

February 16, 2014: Stephen is voted as a starter for his first appearance in an All-Star game

January 9, 2015: Under Armour debuts Stephen Curry's first signature shoe

February 14, 2015: Stephen wins the Three-Point Contest and ranks #1 in votes in 2015 All-Star Weekend

May 4, 2015: Stephen wins NBA MVP award for first time after 2014-15 season.

June 16, 2015: The Warriors win their first championship in 40 years against the Cleveland Cavaliers

July 10, 2015: Daughter Ryan Curry is born

May 10, 2016: Stephen is named unanimous NBA MVP and is the 11th player in NBA history to win the award in consecutive seasons

June 12, 2017: The Warriors win their 2nd NBA championship against the Cleveland Cavaliers

July 1, 2017: Stephen signs a five-year $201 million extension contract with the Warriors and becomes the highest paid NBA player

June 8, 2018: The Warriors win their third championship against the Cleveland Cavaliers.

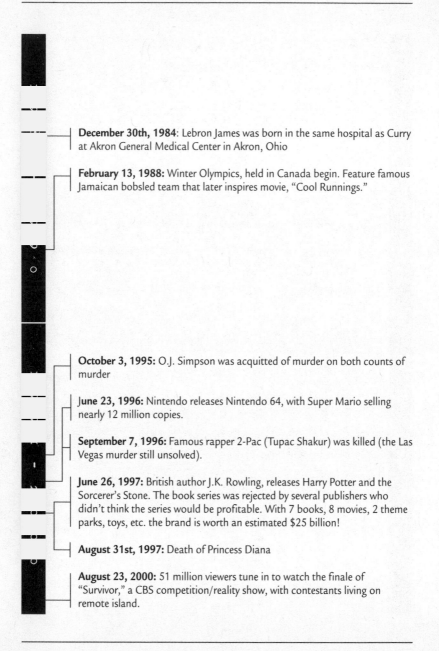

December 30th, 1984: Lebron James was born in the same hospital as Curry at Akron General Medical Center in Akron, Ohio

February 13, 1988: Winter Olympics, held in Canada begin. Feature famous Jamaican bobsled team that later inspires movie, "Cool Runnings."

October 3, 1995: O.J. Simpson was acquitted of murder on both counts of murder

June 23, 1996: Nintendo releases Nintendo 64, with Super Mario selling nearly 12 million copies.

September 7, 1996: Famous rapper 2-Pac (Tupac Shakur) was killed (the Las Vegas murder still unsolved).

June 26, 1997: British author J.K. Rowling, releases Harry Potter and the Sorcerer's Stone. The book series was rejected by several publishers who didn't think the series would be profitable. With 7 books, 8 movies, 2 theme parks, toys, etc. the brand is worth an estimated $25 billion!

August 31st, 1997: Death of Princess Diana

August 23, 2000: 51 million viewers tune in to watch the finale of "Survivor," a CBS competition/reality show, with contestants living on remote island.

January 20, 2001: George W. Bush elected president

September 11, 2001: Islamic terrorist group attacks the United States

February 4, 2004: Facebook was launched

August 23, 2005: Hurricane Katrina hits the Gulf Coast of the U.S, causing over 1,500 fatalities and costing over $125 billion in damage.

March 21, 2006: Twitter goes public. A decade later, the site averages 500 million 'tweets' per day.

September 29, 2008: "The Great Recession," Started in U.S. with drop in home values due to illegal subprime lending. The worst global economic collapse since the Great Depression in the 1930's.

November 4th, 2008: Barack Obama elected president

June 25, 2009: Music and pop-star legend Michael Jackson dies.

April 29, 2011: The Royal wedding between Prince William and Kate Middleton in UK.

December 5, 2013: Former president of South Africa, civil rights leader and philanthropist, Nelson Mandela dies. He had been unjustly held in prison for 27 years, much in solitary confinement. Mandela was released in 1990 and became president in 1994.

October 29th, 2015: China announces the end to their one-child policy after 35 years. Each Chinese family had previously only been allowed to have one child.

November 3, 2016: Chicago Cubs win first World Series since 1908.

July 2, 2018: Stephen and Ayesha Curry announce the birth of their third child and first son, Canon W. Jack Curry.

Becker, Jon. 2017. "The Night Young Stephen Curry Became a Star." *The Mercury News*. March 21. https://www. mercurynews.com/2017/03/21/the-night-young-stephen-curry-became-a-star/.

ESPN. 2013. *Gamecast*. February 28. https://www.espn. com/nba/game?gameId=400278573.

Killion, Ann. 2019. *San Francisco Chronicle*, June 25.

Regna, Michelle. 2016. "Steph And Ayesha Curry's Love Story Will Make Your Heart Hurt." *BuzzFeed*. April 29. https://www.buzzfeed.com/michelleregna/goals-since-day-one?utm_term=.naBX02lqX#.rop39DAM3.

Verry, Peter. 2018. *Footwear News*. February 12. https:// footwearnews.com/2018/focus/athletic-outdoor/stephen-curry-nba-all-star-game-sneakers-under-armour-curry-4-photos-495534/.

Warriors, Golden State. 2009. *NBA.com*. January 1. https://www.nba.com/warriors/photogallery/Draft09_Curry_1.html.

Further Reading

Araton, Harvey. Elevated: *The Global Rise of the N.B.A.* Triumph Books, 2019.

Curcio, Anthony. *The Boy Who Never Gave Up*. CreateSpace, 2016.

Zuckerman, Gregory, Elijah Zuckerman, and Gabriel Zuckerman. Rising Above: *How 11 Athletes Overcame Challenges in Their Youth to Become Stars*. Penguin, New York, 2017.